ALL I NEED TO KNOW,
I Learned Growing Up On a Farm

By JACK ODLE

Designed by Donovan Harris
Edited by Carolyn Garrick Stern

Library of Congress Catalog Number: 97-66629
International Standard Book Number: 08487-2400-3

Table of Contents

Introduction **3**
Courage **8**
Compassion **14**
Responsibility **22**
Patience **30**
Work Ethic **36**
Faith **42**
Love **46**
Honesty **50**
Trust **54**
Life and Death **60**
Rules for Daily Living **66**
Special People, Special Places **68**

Introduction

hen I look at the faded black and white pictures of my grand-parents and great-grandparents, I see the hard work etched in their faces and the stern looks as they posed for the camera. It forces me to think about where I came from, who I am, and how much I owe.

I see other pictures, these of my parents when they were young. I see their laughing faces and cocky looks and wonder in amaze-ment how they could ever have been like that. And in their faces I see a little of me, and I see hints of my children.

I remember old adages about child-rearing that were popular in our house. "Be seen but not heard." "Spare the rod and spoil the child." "If you get in trouble at school, you'll get it

twice as bad when you get home." I remember
these, and now I understand.

I witnessed the impact of humility in action
as I watched my dad get baptized along with
all of us kids. Getting him to church was
always a big event, but getting him to stand in
front of the whole congregation and have
water poured on his head was astounding.
Now, today, I know why.

I learned the importance of giving to others
in their hour of need. It could be a casserole
taken to the home after a funeral or a bucket
of freshly picked apples for a neighbor who
was sick, or it could be combining the wheat

field of a farmer who had been injured.

The cycle of life and death was ever-present. Calves, lambs, pigs, puppies, and kittens were born often right before my eyes. But I also witnessed death and the harshness of nature, all before I was three years old.

I developed patience when I realized there was no way I could speed nature. Everything happens according to nature's schedule, and I can work only within its constraints. I understand now that most times it takes more than just myself to accomplish a task, that hooking up a trailer to the tractor drawbar or sorting cattle in a corral is a lot easier with two.

I know that some things are beyond our control — a bolt of lightning that kills the best cow or a late-season hailstorm that wipes out a crop just before harvest. I know that life doesn't always deal you a hand from the top of the deck. Sometimes things just happen, and you have to adapt and go on. It could be a drought or too much rain or the death of a loved one.

I've seen real men cry, and it's not a pretty sight. They fight it with every ounce of strength they have, but the grief is so powerful it finally breaks through. Even then, the sound isn't loud wailing. It's muffled and sometimes high pitched, and it doesn't last long.

Sometimes there is no sound at all, just a watering of the eyes. But in that brief instant, I learned what real suffering is.

I appreciate the quietness of joy. Joy is almost always tempered as though it might tip life's balance if the celebration is too big. There's a knowledge that happiness is fleeting. Inner peace and understanding of yourself are the important things. It's a happiness that's apparent without being gaudy.

I learned my love for writing from my mom. Every week when I was in college, I got a letter from home. I could hardly wait for the next one. I could read the words and feel the emotion behind the words. I came to under-stand the value and the power of the printed word — of something you could read over and over and still find more meaning.

Yes, just about everything I know worth knowing I learned, and am still learning, from farm families and farm life. I bet a lot of you feel that way too.

Jack Odle

EDITOR,
PROGRESSIVE FARMER

COURAGE

*Adversity comes to all of us —
rich or poor, young or old.
We cannot choose whether it will
come, but we can choose how to
respond to it.*

he day began innocently enough. Dad's tractor wouldn't start, and he wanted me to pull-start him with a second tractor.

This was pretty exciting stuff for a 10-year-old. Mom decided to go along just for the fun of it.

We hooked up the chain. I tried to get my tractor in gear but couldn't even though I had done it before.

Mom decided to help and stepped up on the tractor. Together, we finally got it in gear. Slowly, I eased up on the clutch. The tractor creeped forward, the chain tightened, and Mom jumped. I don't know why she jumped off, but I do know she didn't make it.

The tractor wheel caught her feet, and I watched in horror a scene that has been repeated at least a thousand times since in my mind. The wheel of the small tractor inched up her legs, over her hips, and then down her back and shoulders.

The doctors gave her a 50% chance to live and said she would never walk again. She did live, but Dad had to carry her up steps to basketball games, church, and school events. We were always the first ones there and the last ones to leave.

Then one day, nearly a year after the accident, Mom called to me. Her voice seemed strange and emotional. I went to her immediately.

She was sitting in her wheelchair, smiling. Her eyes were moist and full of love. And then, she stood up.

J.O.

An old cattleman once told me that everyone should go broke at least once; it makes him a better person. He probably meant that the knowledge gained from going broke helps us to be more realistic about ourselves and our values. But he added that he actually had gone broke three times. And he really didn't think he needed all the knowledge he got from going broke twice more!

J.O.

God did not promise us an easy life. He promised that we'd feel good about what we were doing, even when the setbacks came. They came. We feel good.

MARJORIE BUCHANAN, PAWNEE, OKLA.

When beetles killed our pine timber, we sawed the dead wood into lumber and built a broiler house.

STANLEY ROYSTON, CARNESVILLE, GA.

Farmers laugh because they have to.
The tallest tales and funniest stories
grow out of the hardest times.
ROGER WELSCH, DANNEBROG, NEBR.

I like the macho rush I get
from paying accident insurance rates
just ahead of skydivers and soldiers
of fortune.
JIM JOHNSON, COLOGNE, MINN.

COMPASSION

One of the greatest byproducts
of a generous act is that it
inspires more generous acts.
Every person has the ability to
improve the life of someone else.

amily values are getting a lot of press these days. Defining family values gets pretty difficult for some folks. It shouldn't be. Values are shown by simply caring.

I've seen my dad get off his tractor to move a bird's nest out of the way so he could cultivate the field. And I've seen him risk damaging a new combine to help a neighbor.

A mudhole 15 feet wide was right smack in the middle of the gate leading to our neighbor's wheat field. Dad was sitting in front of it on his brand-new combine, revving the engine. Then suddenly he was in the gate, mud flying, the header on the combine barely missing the thick hedge posts. Behind him came two other combines, slipping and sliding, to harvest the 80-acre field for a neighbor, who was recovering from a heart attack.

Dad probably would never have made his valiant charge through that gate with his new combine if the field had been his own.

J.O.

One of the best examples of compassion that I know of comes from a small county few people have ever heard of. For the folks of Chase County, Kans., a 230-pound hog that was sold at the county fair became a symbol of caring.

A few weeks before the fair, Bryan Conley died in a construction accident, leaving two young sons and a wife who was pregnant with their third child. The community grieved, and it found a novel way to show concern.

At the end of the fair every year, 4-H members usually sold one animal in each class of livestock

through an auction. Local merchants, farmers, and livestock producers would buy the animals, usually at an inflated price, and the 4-H members put the money away for college.

That year, a local producer donated a hog to be sold, and the proceeds were to go to the Conley children for their college educations. The hog sold for $2.85 per pound for a total of $655.50. That in itself was amazing enough, but then the buyer *hollered out, "Sell it again."*

They did. In fact, the hog sold 10 more times and raised about $4,000 for the education fund. The reselling of the hog wasn't planned; it was heartfelt and spontaneous. It also came at a time when livestock producers really should have been watching their pennies.

So pat yourself on the back, Chase County. You've shown us how important it is to care about each other. God bless you.

J.O.

Where else can you find five guys willing to listen to your problems every morning at the coffee shop?

CURT AND SUE SAMSON, LAKE CITY, S.D.

I won't mind if my children choose not to farm as long as they have an appreciation for the people who do.

JOHN LIPPS, KINSMAN, OHIO

I see the long furrows filled with crops I have planted and nurtured, and I love knowing that somewhere, somehow, I have helped feed our nation's hungry.

ROGER D. STEVENS, DOTHAN, ALA.

One word of praise will often prevent the need for ten of criticism.

MELVIN D. RUSSELL, COLLIERVILLE, TENN.

The Lord has opened many avenues for me here. And by giving some of the returns from these gifts back through charitable work, I hope to open new paths for others to follow.

ADAM NIETO, VEGA, TEX.

RESPONSIBILITY

On the farm, everybody has a job. And if it's not done, the results show up pretty quickly.

up was a terrier/bird-dog cross of some kind. He loved to go rabbit hunting, tolerated bird hunting, and wouldn't work cattle worth a darn. It is this last trait that makes my story so unusual.

Our family went to a high school baseball game one afternoon. When we returned late that night, we heard barking down near the hay shed. We found Pup there, holding six cows and their calves inside.

The cattle had gotten out of the corral, and apparently Pup decided they needed to stay put until we got back. He had never done anything like that before, and he never did it again. Still, thanks to this one responsible act, Pup has gone down in Odle family dog lore.

J.O.

Taking care of the land is a duty that today's farmers and ranchers don't take lightly. But there seems to be an environmental feeding frenzy going on, with technology as the scapegoat. Consumers are getting mixed messages from environmental groups.

Christmas tree farmers are blasted for using chemicals and fuel to grow trees. But these real trees, unlike artificial Christmas trees, are natural and will degrade. So a consumer either

buys a plastic tree, which uses oil in the manufacturing process and which never degrades, or buys a real tree that has been treated with pesticides but will degrade. Another choice, I guess, is to cancel Christmas.

J.O.

When my daughter was younger, I spent a Saturday morning watching cartoons with her. Honest, I did this as research. I wanted to see how many times scientists and researchers are depicted as evil.

We watched six cartoon shows, and in five of them the scientists were the bad guys. No wonder it's hard to get kids interested in science.

Which cartoon didn't depict a scientist as evil? Popeye. And he has a friend named Wimpy who consumes bushels of hamburgers, which we're constantly being told are bad for us.

J.O.

On rainy days, my grandfather would take an umbrella in one hand and a hedge knife in the other and go cut weeds. He called it "improving the quality of time."

EARL THORP, CLINTON, ILL.

We never asked to be rich or to have prestige, but we have indeed been blessed. We have three children who we hope will give back to the world more than they'll ever take from it.

VINSON AND MARY ANN ICENHOUR, TAYLORSVILLE, N.C.

Our children know that you reap as you sow, that there are no shortcuts to doing things right, and that there are natural consequences to our actions.

GAILEN BRIDGES, INDEPENDENCE, KY.

The greatest gift we can give to the next generation is the opportunity to learn from their own experience.

DAN LOGAN, GILLIAM, LA.

PATIENCE

Patience is nothing more and nothing less than constructive waiting.

ow many times have you knelt beside a row and, using your hand, carefully dug into the dirt to see whether the seed had begun to sprout? You know you can't hurry the progress; you're just curious.

J.O.

In a world where everyone is in such a hurry and people are going in a thousand different directions, it's satisfying to know that you can't hurry the grass or corn into growing or speed the birth of a calf.

ALLISON S. RAMSEY, PERRYVILLE, KY.

I eventually learned that the final pull on a large crescent wrench will usually end with a loud snap.

STANLEY SHAVLIK, LINWOOD, NEBR.

I get a kick out of the ritual of cutting hay to make the rain start.

BETH LANTGEN, ESTELLINE, S.D.

I have my explanation for why I farm down pat because I've been married to the same woman for 30 years, and I've had lots of practice explaining.

DONNIE HILL, KINGSTON, TENN.

Patience is having a son,
a son-in-law, and a hired man all
working on your farm.
HOMER FERGUSON, OSKALOOSA, IOWA

I like the challenge of keeping cool
when, after working outdoors next to
my husband all morning, I walk into the
house with him and he says,
"Is dinner ready?"
MARY ANN CUKA, TYNDALL, S.D.

Weather, markets, disease, and
equipment problems all require me
to bend, adapt, and change according to
the situation. Planning is difficult
and often reduced to taking
one day at a time.

R. KELLY COFFEY, BOONE, N.C.

WORK ETHIC

A farmer was once asked whether he had been farming all his life. He replied, "Not yet, I ain't." His wry answer told a lot about his sense of humor, and it also held a deeper meaning. He wasn't through living. He still had challenges to face and to overcome.

I remember looking out
at a field full of hay bales
and wondering if we would
ever get them loaded and
hauled to the barn.

I came to realize that if you work
steadily and stick to it, those bales will
slowly disappear from the field.

J.O.

Nothing stimulates new ideas
like friendly competition with a
good neighbor.

EARL GARBER, IOTA, LA.

I've learned that cussing at machinery
always helps.

DONNA KAMPMEIER, CHOKIO, MINN.

Don't keep telling me what I need to know. Why, there's already an awful gap between what I know and what I do.

MITCHELL LYND, JOHNSTOWN, OHIO

I've worked other jobs. These jobs were what I did. A farmer is what I am.

GEORGE H. WIEMERS, GREENVIEW, ILL.

Goals don't become concrete until you write them down.

PAT LICHTER, MONTROSE, MO.

Just as an artist endeavors to paint a better picture each time, we strive to do our best in farming each year.

CHALMERS AND BETTY WHITCHER
SOUTH PITTSBURG, TENN.

I have tried singing in the tractor cab along with the radio, but it sounds terrible.

WARD SCOTT, FARRAGUT, IOWA

Finding happiness in duty is one of life's great joys.

L.H. "COTTON" IVY, DECATUR COUNTY, TENN.

FAITH

Farming takes a lot of faith,
faith in yourself and in the
nature of things.

’ve watched the planting of tiny seed and had the assurance that they would sprout and make a good crop. I've watched a newborn calf struggle to its feet and understood this fragile animal would grow into a productive cow.

Those who farm or raise livestock have the advantage of seeing miracles happen every day.

J.O.

Worry is the opposite of faith. At its worst, worry is a debilitating disease. It affects the way you think, the way you move, the way you view others, and the way you view yourself.

It grasps you and holds you in a state of limbo and prevents you from making decisions or taking positive actions. At its best, worry is a waste of time.

J.O.

Don't worry — we're a lot like chickens. We thrive best when we have to scratch a little for what we get.

FRED G. PRINCE, NEW ALBANY, MISS.

This is a great "next year" country.

DAN WHITE, VERNON, TEXAS

The closeness of nature and all the rewards of the heart bring us closer to God. What better way to see the work of God than through the eyes of the farmer.

BRENDA ENGLISH, LEXINGTON, N.C.

Through all of the years of raising family, crops, and hogs, our faith sustained us, and we never seemed to worry about the droughts and weeds.

JEAN PRULL, MONTICELLO, IOWA

LOVE

You can feel love in hands
worn rough by seasons of
gathering and preserving food
and soothing hurts.
It's the emotion that helps us get
up in the morning, keeps us going,
and makes us smile.

ne Christmas, our family decided not to buy gifts for each other. Instead, we shared a part of ourselves by giving time or gifts we made. For instance, I committed the time to landscape into our backyard a flower garden specifically for my wife.

The flowers weren't planted until spring, of course, except for the tulips. The garden is something we both tend together and will last for years.

For my daughter, I prepared a notebook — actually it's a diary — of my thoughts about her birth,

her first birthday, when she first walked, her first words, and the like. I update it every so often, and when she becomes a teenager I'll give it to her. Of course, she got some gifts she could enjoy at Christmas too.

My parents received a photo album depicting their granddaughter, arrayed and disarrayed in all her glory. This was our small effort to emphasize the real reason for the holiday.

J.O.

Working the ground my grandfather and father worked leaves me with a feeling of touching their dreams.

Don and Linda Hildebrand, LaMoille, Ill.

Being a farmer you know your wife married you because she loves you and not your money.

Phyllis Quincy, Platteville, Wis.

The way you raise your family, the quality of a marriage, the time spent with family and friends; these are ways to measure success.

Randy E. Haddock, Attica, Ind.

HONESTY

Every time you lie, a small piece of you dies. Those who make lying a practice soon don't know who they are. It's better to point out the lame heifer to a buyer rather than wait for the buyer to find her in the herd — or worse, not find her.

hen I was in high school, I learned a valuable lesson about honesty. A friend and I were goofing around, and we got to school late. We told our teacher that we had had a flat tire and that it took a while to change it.

She immediately had us sit down, and she told us we were going to take a test. The test would have only one question, and we couldn't look at each other's answer. The question was, "Which tire was flat?"

J.O.

Liars need to have darn good memories. I'll never be a good liar because I can't remember anything I said five minutes after I said it.
HAROLD ODLE

My friends and I worked for my dad, and he worked us hard enough that we were too tired to get into trouble.

But we just seemed to know what was right and what was wrong, not that we always did the right thing.
JOHN LIPPS, KINSMAN, OHIO

I farm because my land is too far from town for a parking lot and too flat for a golf course.

DICK HOUSE, ARTHUR, ILL.

TRUST

Americans are great at building high-rise condos, super-highways, and spaceships. What we're not doing so well is creating credibility among ourselves.

---

haracter counts in agriculture. I learned that a man's word is his bond; that a handshake is a contract. And that you don't do business with people you don't trust.

J.O.

"Daddy, Daddy, catch me,"
my three-year-old son Johnny
yelled just before he jumped
into my arms at the
swimming pool.

J.O.

I wouldn't be farming today
without the help of my two friends.
They helped me get started when I had
no money to buy equipment.
KEITH THOMPSON, RUSSELL COUNTY, ALA.

When we took the plunge and
abandoned the security of a weekly
paycheck, we threw away the
alarm clock.
ALLISON CLIMER, BELLS, TENN.

We don't need an ATM in our town because the local cafe will cash a check for as much as our bank account will bear.

CONNIE HANSEN, ANSELMO, NEBR.

One of the greatest rewards of being a farmer is the neighbors who come with the farm. Neighbors lend a helping hand when you need it. They can be depended on and confided in, and they are your best friends.

GARTH JORDAN, OSAGE, IOWA

LIFE AND DEATH

Some folks save it,
others make it, most waste it,
several kill it, and a few actually
are on it. Many try to manage it
and end up losing it. Time is a
taker. Once past, it never returns.
How it's spent determines the
satisfaction of life.

 aising kids on concrete doesn't always work well. Children need to get their hands dirty, smell fresh-turned earth, sweat a little, and experience the joy and excitement of witnessing a tiny plant shoot emerge from the soil.

To understand nature, to appreciate nature, children need to be close to it. Also, spending time in the country gives children the freedom to romp, explore, and enjoy nature's treasures. And those special moments, either in a make-believe world of cowboys and Indians or in the real world walking through a pasture with parents, help build character and instill strong values in young minds.

You get a different perspective on life when you share it with a young person. Children look at the world through new eyes, and they force those around them to do the same. When my daughter Katie was three years old, she saw a butterfly sitting on a daisy. The butterfly lifted itself from the flower and came gliding over her head. Katie said, "Look, Daddy, the flower is flying!"

But life's riches don't come only from the young and active. I treasure the moments I've spent with older people too. We featured Rufus Brasher in our February 1986 centennial anniversary issue. At the time, he was 103 years old and his wife, Mae, was 100. Rufus, who lived nearly two lifetimes, died in January 1987. He was a key to our past, a reminder of our responsibilities to the present, and a look at our future.

Rufus taught each of us at *Progressive Farmer* something. One of his statements will stick with me for the rest of my life: "People are in just too big a rush nowadays. They need to slow down and get to know each other."

J. O.

Farming keeps my feet planted in the ground, and it teaches me the laws of life.

PERRY W. BLACKWELL, TYLERTOWN, MISS.

At my grandfather's funeral, I cried more for myself than for him. I cried because of the necessary cycles in nature and youth and growing up, which often separate us from one another. And I mourned that I probably lost Papa the day I became too old to spend a summer afternoon catching crawdaddies with him.

LEAH SWEARINGEN, SAN DIEGO, CALIF.

I have always said that I hoped
we could retire at least by the time we
reached 70. But the older I get,
the younger that seems. Maybe I'll just
retire when I die.

AMY SHARPE FITTS, SILER CITY, N.C.

Never have I looked back and
wished for a different life. Bad times and
good times were stepping stones to a
more rewarding life.

LILLIE RICHMOND, BLANKET, TEXAS

We will never have to build that nest egg so that we can someday move to the country. We're already here!

KATHY HENNINGS, WAUSA, NEBR.

Grandmother's recipes and hand-sewn quilts and Mother's unconditional love were all left to us for comfort and joy to soothe our troubled souls.

We sometimes sit on the old porch swing where generations of Stewarts have sat. We gaze across the farm at sunset after a hard day's toil, and we hear the whispers of those Stewarts long gone that seem to say, "A day's work well done."

JAMES AND LINDA STEWART, GREENUP, ILL.

Rules For Daily Living

From **Progressive Farmer** *in the late 1950's*

☞ To be strong in the presence of temptation, awake in the presence of opportunity, open-hearted to my neighbors, obedient to the calls of good conscience, open-minded to the views of Truth.

☞ To make duty a joy and work a duty.

☞ To work and not worry; to be energetic without being fussy.

☞ To be true to myself, false to no one, and earnest to make a real life while trying to make a living.

☞ To cherish friendships and guard my confidences.

☞ To be loyal to principle even at the loss of popularity.

☞ To make no promises I do not mean to keep and few of them.

☞ To be faithful to every honest obligation.

☞ To be respectful, not cringing, to the great; gentle to the weak; helpful to the fallen; courteous to all.

Special People, Special Places

In case you know someone who has trouble telling the difference between city and country living, I have a number of surefire indicators. Most were sent to me by people like you who have a good handle on what makes farm and small-town living so special.

J. O.

Rural is . . .

🖙 Where everybody knows your name and why your mother named you that.

🖙 Where everybody knows your dog's name.

🖙 Where there is only a four-digit difference between your home telephone number, your doctor's number, and your work number.

🌿 Where your dog knows everyone in town.

🌿 Where the "new" releases at the local theater come after the movie is already on videocassette tape.

🌿 Where the church bulletin publishes the community activities: who will operate the concession stand, the date of the next volunteer fire department meeting, and who will referee the basketball game.

🌿 Where you don't use your turn signal because everyone knows where you're going.

🌿 Where you write a check on the wrong bank, and they cover for you.

🌿 Where you miss a Sunday at church and get six "get well" cards.

🌿 Where you dial the wrong number and talk for 15 minutes anyway.

Special thanks . . .
to all the *Progressive Farmer* readers
who have taken the time to share their
thoughts about country life with us.

PRODUCTS DIVISION

For additional copies of *All I Need To Know,
I Learned Growing Up on a Farm,* send a
check or money order for $7.95 per book
(including shipping and handling) to Box
830069, Birmingham, AL 35283-0069. For
credit card orders, call 1-800-425-0374.